The Fireside Book

A picture and a poem for every mood
chosen by

David Hope

Published by D.C. THOMSON & CO., LTD.,
185 Fleet Street, LONDON EC4A 2HS. © D.C. Thomson & Co., Ltd., 2011

DC Thomson

CONTENTS

SEPTEMBER SONG

A TOUCH of autumn in the air,
The clouds go sailing through the sky,
Brown leaves appearing here and there,
And time and tide flow swiftly by.

The scent of wood smoke on the breeze,
A skein of wild geese overhead,
The evening sun lights fields and trees
And turns the world to pink and red.

All nature has a perfect plan,
A special magic to impart,
So catch the wonder when you can,
And keep September in your heart.

Iris Hesselden

9

LOVE IS . . .

**LOVE is . . .
Fragile as cobwebs,
Tempered as steel.
Fabric of dreamtime,
All that is real.
Desired beyond diamonds
Yet freely bestowed,
Light to illumine
Life's perilous road.
Small glow of comfort,
Beacon of hope,
Reason for tying
A knot in the rope.
Giving, forgiving
Whatever the cost,
A haven awaiting
The lonely and lost.
Raising the heart
with magical leaven,
Song of the Earth,
Echo of Heaven.**

Tricia Sturgeon

THE SALMON'S RETURN

THEY nose the estuaries
All the power of their length
Bent on remembering, conquering,
Reaching, finding.

The water is deep,
So cold it is sore as the plunging of knife.
The water is loud with autumn, brash and chattering,
Rushing seaward with news of colours and fires.

The salmon flicker upwards, loom through pools.
Gashing themselves on giant boulders,
Before pausing, halted, at the feet of the falls.

The water comes in whisky, clatters
Like an old man falling, rolling, heedless
Down a staircase. The salmon
Hurl, thrash, fist upwards at the sky,
Out of their element, arch taut and driven until
They win, calm water, shallow quiet.

Then they are almost home,
Their mouths tasting the roots of the hills
They unravelled, they followed
From the light blue salt of the Atlantic
All the way back, to this beginning.

Kenneth C. Steven

ENCOUNTER

AS snowflakes fluttered gently down
And settled on the ground,
I ventured forth on slippered feet
Softly without sound.
For there within a pool of light
Beneath the lamppost's glow,
There stood a little golden fox
Staring at the snow.

He stood quite still as if entranced —
Of my presence unaware,
But then he turned and caught my gaze
And quietly sniffed the air.
Then stealthily he slunk away
Into the snowy night,
But this encounter filled my heart
With wonder and delight.

Kathleen Gillum

VISIT WOODLAND

VISIT woodland — yes, today!
Pack a bag, get up and go.
Ditch appointments — don't delay,
catch the great autumnal show.

Overnight, the woodlands turn
to umber, orange, scarlet, brown.
All at once the bushes burn,
all at once the leaves come down.

Looping, swooping, falling, stalling,
reeling, wheeling, blazing, amazing!
Earthwards gliding, thermal riding,
whirling, twirling, senses fazing.

Visit woodland — make it soon.
Join the great autumnal ball.
Leaves dance to the breeze's tune.
Come — succumb to beauty's thrall.

Janet McKenzie

GOLD

GOD grants us gifts of golden things;
Gold morning light, gold-leaf on songbirds' wings.
Buttercups' random gold through field and hedge,
Coltsfoot clip-clopping down to summer's edge.
Pale gold of flaxen hair, autumn's brief rage.
The gleaming topaz of a cat's cool gaze.
Swift-garnered treasury of harvest time.
The gilded resonance of church bells' chime —
And traced among life's variegated page,
Gold dust of memories to soothe old age.

Joan Howes

ACQUAINTED WITH AUTUMN

I SKIRTED scarlet oak and beech for miles,
their brilliant cloaks hemmed crookedly with fence,
and followed where the farmer paved an aisle
of fields aglow with fallen opulence,
releasing row on row of redolence.
Sumac blushed as though to signify
autumn's crimson kiss upon the day;
and suddenly, from wild grasses high,
a slender hind stepped out into my way
and stopped, eyes bright, then nimbly slipped away.

Rachel Wallace-Oberle

CLOCKS AWAY!

TODAY'S the day the clocks go back,
Well, that's good news for sure –
I'll be an hour younger than
I was the day before!
And should the powers-that-be decide
To turn back Time each week,
I'd soon be really young again,
And fit, and at my peak.
But oh – when springtime comes around
And clocks must forward go,
I might just shrivel like a leaf,
My hair turn white as snow.
So no, let's leave things as they are –
At least we've naught to fear
While clocks change but an hour a day
And only twice a year!

Margaret Ingall

23

SECRETS OF
THE NIGHT

WHEN at last the day is done
and long the shadows fall,
Flowers close their petals
that grace the garden wall.
Everywhere is stillness
cloaked in a velvet gown,
Birds have settled in their nests
of twigs and thistledown.
Now everywhere seems quiet,
a time for sweet repose,
A slumber overwhelming,
or so one would suppose.
But in woodland nooks and crannies
little creatures stir,
And go about their business
by bush and conifer.
Owls and bats have taken flight
on noiseless beating wings,
As gentle summer breezes
make leafy murmurings.
Such are the many mysteries
that intrigue and delight,
In the mystic wonderland
of secrets of the night.

Brian H. Gent

THE STREAM

IT never ceases to thrill,
  watching it narrowly race,
or spread wider, shallow, and almost still,
or rippling like a badly-painted
wall, or from some hogback
height implode upon itself.
Beneath the bridge its tidemark
shoulder buffs a smooth shelf,
old as experience, and as I watch,
familiar Pooh-sticks hurry past
in the swirl of memory's mist,
too swift, too swift to catch.

John Ellis

SEASONAL WISDOM

WHEN I was young, I knew I was immortal,
Sure age would simply nod, and pass me by.
Mind and body ne'er would fail or falter,
And Time held but the whisper of a sigh.

Sweet youth's illusions lasted all through summer,
And even autumn held them for a while.
But here is winter, wrapping me in silver,
And, strange to tell, I really like the style.

For now I see beyond the smoke and mirrors,
And know the wheel is turning, as it should,
So that the heart may choose its dearest treasures
With which to clothe the soul for ill or good.

Tricia Sturgeon

HEBRIDEAN REFLECTIONS

EVEN at midsummer the wind is always there;
A chasing sky; grass beaten flat,
Gulls bending through torn blue sky,
And somewhere a washing line flapping with clothes,
Thrashing the wind, as if waving
To all the sons who left these islands,
Who were blown overseas at the mercy of gales –
The storms' history –
And never returned.

Kenneth Steven

WINTER LIMES

ON winter limes a lens
of slenderest sunlight plays,
turning bark to bronze
in early morning's haze.

From skeletal branches grow,
like gourds of alluring fruit,
sperules of mistletoe,
too high to harvest.

Around the tawny boles,
anklets of mirrored sunrise,
untimely daffodils,
scene stealers on bare canvas.

Raucous and quarrelsome,
crows in their unroofed haven
rasp rowdy welcome
to the red-eyed dawn.

John Ellis

33

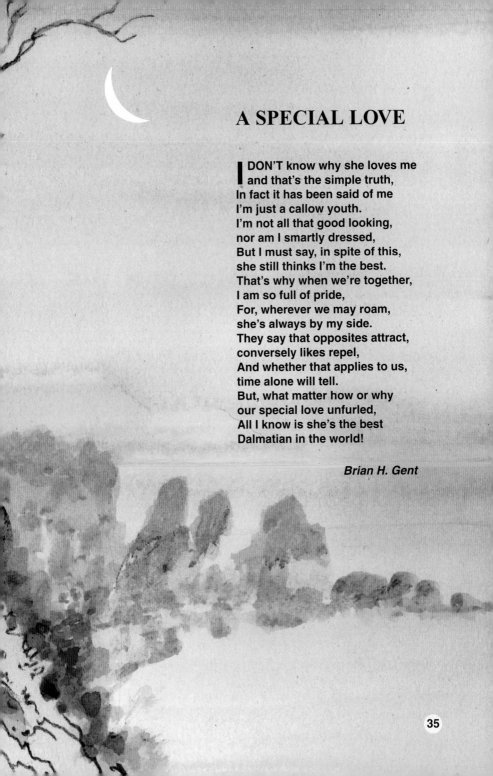

A SPECIAL LOVE

I DON'T know why she loves me
and that's the simple truth,
In fact it has been said of me
I'm just a callow youth.
I'm not all that good looking,
nor am I smartly dressed,
But I must say, in spite of this,
she still thinks I'm the best.
That's why when we're together,
I am so full of pride,
For, wherever we may roam,
she's always by my side.
They say that opposites attract,
conversely likes repel,
And whether that applies to us,
time alone will tell.
But, what matter how or why
our special love unfurled,
All I know is she's the best
Dalmatian in the world!

Brian H. Gent

YIPPEE!

NEW YEAR'S DAY — I stop and stand.
Young otters hump across the sand
tumbling, teasing as they run
chasing each other to the sea
quite uninhibited by me;
three little otters having fun.
They look so gloriously at home
in salty spray and curling foam,
so exuberantly alive.
Uplifted by their antics there,
I see black nostrils sip the air,
watch them surf the breakers, dive.
"Yippee!" I dream I hear them say,
"Come on in! It's New Year's Day."

Iain Dubh

BIRCH IN WINTER

I SAW the birch as evening fell,
sketched within a wintry spell,
and stopped among their long-sleeved limbs —
graceful arches, pale and slim —
that cast aside their garments old
in defiance of the cold.
Across the freshly fallen snow
like scattered strips of calico,
stiffly frilled discarded cloaks
of those stately silent folk,
scuffled with an icy wind
and then were gone, surrendering.

Rachel Wallace-Oberle

THE ELFIN FAIR

TRUMPET or drum,
trumpet or drum,
is carried in every hand,
as throngs of dancing fairies come
to follow the elfin band.

Two by two,
such a hullabaloo,
as the Queen comes into the square,
sitting aloft on the back of a shrew,
to open the elfin fair.

In the night sky,
the moon rides high
above the enchanted woods,
where stalls lit up by firefly
are laden with fairy goods.

40

Come young, come old,
one hundredfold,
in yellow, green, or red,
all will exchange some fairy gold
for elfin gingerbread.

And, not to be mean,
the elfin Queen
rewards her elfin band,
with a jug or two of best poteen,
at the fair in Elfinland.

John Ellis

DRY DOCK

IT has always been so, once the weather improves:
a huddle of men gather, staring down into the harbour.
Today, a clamp is being attached to a boat,
and the "Fulmar" starts to wobble.
Half in, half out of the water, yet still afloat
swinging unsteadily, she is lifted high, turned
around, placed on a lorry and made secure, then
driven off to an inland sanctuary. More boats
are hauled up, set in stocks along the quay
like sitting ducks waiting to be scraped and buffed
right down to the carcase.

Only the "Island Queen" remains haughtily resplendent.
The rest, on terra firma, wait
to be painted, kitted out in cobalt, emerald and scarlet,
lovingly inscribed, refreshed for baptism on strong spring
tides.
Then "Lena", "Giselle", "Crusader", "Bay Fisher" will rejoin
that crooked old rogue the crimson "Enchanter",
a lopsided lump of timber which lies at an angle
like a basking shark or a lazy lizard,
blinking into the sun.

Ruth Walker

43

WINTER SPRITE

THE silhouettes of leafless trees
Are etched against the sky,
With branches spread like outstretched arms
Forever reaching high.
The ebony of bark and bough
Is bathed in pearly light,
As silver frost like tinselled thread
Is glistening clear and bright.

It seems as if a winter sprite
All dressed in frozen rime,
Has woven with an icy hand
An intricate design.
By scattering his fairy dust
On every naked tree,
Has clothed each branch and bough and twig
In jewelled embroidery.

Kathleen Gillum

PHOTO OF A DEAR FRIEND

I SAW a photograph of you, the other day,
Taken, oh some many years ago.
You must have been . . . about sixteen, I'd say,
And all alight with youth's intrinsic glow.

Gazing from that sepia tinted page,
You faced the years, advancing one by one,
Not heeding winter's waiting grey-meshed cage
Nor worried spring's bright bloom must soon be gone.

And rightly so. For all that Time could do
To show his footprints marching through the years,
Was mark his presence with a line or two
Recording, "Here was laughter", "Here were tears."

That photograph I saw, the other day
Was very lovely but, its day is done.
And I prefer your present countenance,
For all I love in you, is writ thereon.

Tricia Sturgeon

WINTER!

SNOWFLAKES in thousands, are here for a visit,
Creaming the hedgerows, adorning the trees;
Chaining like collars of diamond on twiglet,
Flailing the air, to prepare for the freeze!

Lightness and shadow in symmetry mingle,
Silhouette casting a delicate grace;
Beauty embalmed in a statuesque posing,
Filigree patterns a web of white lace.

Icicle coronets garland the windows,
Frost points a lattice, no hand could array;
Though worlds may triumph with wonders of science,
Nature decides how long winter will stay!

Elizabeth Gozney

ICE-BREAKERS

OVERNIGHT the canal froze,
Its surface glassing
Into a long contact lens of ice.
Everything went static;
The ducks stood by
In unemployed groups;
The water vole waited,
Watched, speculated;
And the kingfisher's blue
Got stolen away.

But in a small corner
Still touched
By the February sun,
A cob and pen
Set out to cut a path,
Breaking the ice
With slow-burning energy,
Returning the canal
To shimmering life,
Shimmering light.

David Elder

FEBRUARY THOUGHTS

A TIME of looking forward
As winter slips away,
The crocus lifts her cheerful head
And there's a longer day.
The New Year lies behind us
Our resolutions gone,
But we will cherish hopes and dreams
As time keeps moving on.

And soon March winds will herald spring,
Soft green touch every tree,
The daffodils will sway and dance,
A joy for all to see.
But until then, though frost and fog
Spread February gloom,
Be optimistic in your heart
And watch the springtime bloom.

Iris Hesselden

53

THE GOOD MORNING

FAIR maids of February straight and bright as hope,
no less-fine day could spring you from the earth.
Diamond stars scored out from night's black pane
this morning's slice-of-melon moon. Cat-ice
crinkles shallows at the loch's curved edge
like wrinkles round an old, fond, smiling, mouth.
Reeds frocked by frost. Sea, poussin-blue on blue.
Sunlight glistening from mica in the schist.
Breeze steals on tiptoe, breath held, giggling, plays
Grandmother's Footsteps, or some such nursery game.
Road dry as wit. Air fragile. Sugar crisp,
beneath a golden fringe of glorying cloud
curled tightly as a painted angel's hair,
far island hills distinct as innocence.

Iain Dubh

THIS DAY

THIS day is mine, sings the skylark
as she soars from her nest in the dawn.
Mine is the silver-tipped sunrise,
the trembling of morning scarce born.

This day is mine, sniffs the rabbit,
as he wrinkles his nose at the breeze.
The tang of the earth, damp and dewy,
the scent of the lace-blossomed trees.

This day is mine, knows the roe deer,
alert to each feeling, each sound.
The whisper of leaves in the woodland,
the snap of each twig on the ground.

"This day was mine," says the traveller,
"Yes, even if days dawn no more."
And he smiles as he turns his step homeward,
and follows the path to his door.

Margaret Ingall

THE FROGS' RETURN

I HEARD a whirling like a far-off
Water wheel. I stood,
I watched the water —
Nothing here it seemed
So I tracked the sound until
At last, I found,
Hidden in brown reeds,
Frogs! Great numbers had returned.
My heart throbbed with
The gurgling noise,
My head felt light,
The frogs were back
And they had brought the spring.

Jenny Whybrow

SPARKLE

I ONLY caught a sparkle
From the corner of my eye,
The merest little twinkle, but
I knew they were close by,
Polishing the sunbeams
To keep them looking new,
Collecting vacant cobwebs
All dazzling with dew.
Dusting off the daisies
So they're ready for the fray,
And tucking up the stars to sleep
Throughout the whole long day.

These tiny little elfin folk
So magical and wise,
Are all around about us,
Tho' often in disguise.
They'll hide behind a buttercup,
A lupin or a rose,
Sheltered there so snugly
You can't even see their toes.
So, though you may not spy them
Oh, never have a doubt,
A sparkle or a tinkle means
That fairies are about.

Tricia Sturgeon

SPRING GARLAND

WHITE is the May.
Sad willows come to leaf
And all our wasted grief
Turns wistfully away.

Lilac dips low.
Tears we need not have shed
Lie in a winter bed
Beneath the cherry snow.

Laburnums dance.
Dispelling tides of care
With locks of yellow hair
Tossed in exuberance.

Daisies delight.
While melancholy things
From long forgotten springs
Are turned to joyous flight.

White is the May.
Happiness held in trust,
Stippled with petal dust —
Care's cobwebs cast away.

Joan Howes

A FIELD IN FIFE

THE field has been unearthed by the plough
Lies black and ribbed, rises to a ridge of hillside.
Winter bites the air, a blue-white cold;
I clamber up the ridge and stand, breathless,
The Tay a stretch of grey-blue dark below —
Beyond, the glens of Angus feathered still with snow.
My hands hurt. For hours we wander the field
As though looking for something lost, picking
At bits of crystal — amethyst and smoky quartz —
And the orange ripeness of carnelian.
Sometimes, just sometimes, we find agates —
Moon-dimpled, big as our fists and bigger,
Filled inside with rings like cut trees.

Kenneth Steven

PORTRAIT OF SPRING

SHOW me the woods and meadows,
The gentle rolling downs:
The spreading hills and valleys,
The pastel greens and browns.

Give me the chance to wander
The rambling country lanes,
And feel the fleeting showers
of springtime's refreshing rains.

Then to a friendly cottage
For a welcome cup of tea
Where the breath of new bread baking
Brings my childhood back to me!

Handful of precious memories
I'll take with me where I roam,
For deep in my heart I know that —
Memories bring thoughts of home.

Elizabeth Gozney

FAERY LAND

LIKE green curtains
  The honeysuckle trails around
The windows of the silver boughs
And the sun sends tiny faery jewels
Of translucent light.
A small bird peers
Through lichened leaves and
The year's first bumble bee,
In honied gold
Dances in the warmth of spring's
Soft breath.

Jenny Whybrow

SEAL AT KINTYRE

STUMBLING from the sun-warm sand,
I shiver in the sudden chill
thrill of the sea's embrace.

I lean on ocean, drift from land,
I turn my head and, by my side,
wide-eyed, a winsome face.

A surface ripple laps my hand.
I turn my head and, by my side,
wide-eyed, a winsome face.

We gaze at one another, and
it seems as if the world's on hold –
bold looks make pulses race.

He vanishes – a dimple's trace
recording meeting filled with grace.

Janet McKenzie

BENISON

WHITE doves plumping and preening on the roof,
black hens crooning, tut-tutting beneath.
A string of onions drying out on a washing pole,
in a long hot summer of lazy afternoons.
Bramley apples, almost ready to drop
to the grass, sure prey for birds, or wasps.

Watering cans waiting for rain,
a smothering of roses, fairly
covering an ancient garden seat.
A winding path of paving stones
luring the eye beyond the front door,
the step, the grating for muddy boots.

A wheelbarrow, with a spade plunged
into a potato trench, the sweet reek
of the bonfire catching one's throat;
a cool mist rolling in from the sea
the promise of the returning sun.

Ruth Walker

LUPIN

ALONG the edge of town the lupin grows
and trims the path in slender brilliant rows,
bearing bells that reach out for the breeze
and bend in lovely purple arcs; oh, these
are Nature's glorious parentheses!
As birds call out I walk the path, forlorn
and kneel to gather spires, crushed and torn;
in the mowing, wild grasses sweet fell
and in the heady fragrant heat
the lupin pours its perfume at my feet.

Rachel Wallace-Oberle

A RED, RED ROSE

OH my luve is like a red, red rose,
That's newly sprung in June:
Oh my luve is like the melodie,
That's sweetly play'd in tune.

As fair art thou, my bonnie lass,
So deep in luve I am;
And I will luve thee still, my dear,
Till a' the seas gang dry.

Till a' the seas gang dry my dear,
And the rocks melt wi' the sun;
And I will luve thee still, my dear,
While the sands o' life shall run.

And fare thee weel, my only luve!
And fare thee weel a while!
And I will come again, my luve,
Tho' it were ten thousand mile!

Robert Burns

WILLOW COTTAGE

THIS was the fabric of a long-held dream,
Epitomised in wood and slumbering stone.
Warm with the gentle breath of passing years,
Fragrant with ancient herbage, softly grown
In the unhurried mists of long-ago,
When Time, more frail than thought, paused at the door
And left no mark, beyond vague mellowing
Of rose-toned brick, blurred bands of timbering
And spendthrift light, spilled on a shadowed floor.
This garden knew the tread of distant feet,
Whose prints still rest on history's tapestry.
These roses felt the touch of bygone hands,
Now linked in one immense eternity.
All those who laughed or wept within these walls
Have left some stain of self to whisper here,
Weaving a web of presence, loosely hung
Upon the dwindling frame of yesteryear.

Joan Howes

BUTTERCUP BOWER

AS I look out on fields of gold
Contrasting skies of blue
I sense there's magic in the day
For all seems fresh and new.
Vivid, vital yellow flowers
With sunny vibrancy
Are stretching out before me now
Far as the eye can see.

It seems a sea of sunshine has
Been spread for my delight
Alive and bold and beautiful
All colourful and bright.
My heart leaps up and wants to dance
I'm filled with energy
Just gazing at this wondrous scene
That's captivating me.

As dormant feelings spring to life
I feel my spirits rise
Responding to the beauty
That is there before my eyes.
Filled with hope I raise my face
To feel the sun's warm kiss
For everything seems possible
On such a day as this.

Kathleen Gillum

SUNSET OVER THE SEA . . .

WATCHING the sun setting over the sea
Words can hardly express,
The breathtaking view of scarlet and gold,
Brilliant and fiery, striking and bold;
Colourful splendour etched to impress —
Sun setting over the sea!

Nature defies any artist to paint
An image, to truly convey,
The sunbeam flaming a path o'er the deep,
and making the ripples, as though they would leap;
Reflecting the sky, at the close of the day —
Sun setting over the sea!

Elizabeth Gozney

THE GARDEN

A WINDING crazy-paving path
  edged with aubretia's hues,
Leads down to the summer house,
to phlox and feverfews,
Pink briar roses tumble
along the old stone wall,
And when the grasses turn bright green,
laburnum tassels fall,
In a pond where moss and lichen
decorate the rim,
A little fountain patters
and goldfish languid swim,
A pewter-grey sundial
records the passing day,
With all the changing patterns
of the garden's roundelay.

Brian H. Gent

THE MAY PATH

I KNOW a place where
hundreds of archangels
don golden halos to enhance
spring's dullest day;
where a crashed sky of bluebells,
dense-wrecked among the trees,
leaks into the woodland way
an ecstasy of fragrance;
and where in May
myriads of ramsons stir
like a sea of snowflake crystals,
drowning the very air
in fitful tsunamis
of their pungent essence.

John Ellis

SHE WALKS IN BEAUTY

SHE walks in beauty, like the night
Of cloudless climes and starry skies;
And all that's best of dark and bright
Meet in her aspect and her eyes:
Thus mellow'd to that tender light
Which heaven to gaudy day denies.

One shade the more, one ray the less,
Had half impair'd the nameless grace
Which waves in every raven tress,
Or softly lightens o'er her face;
Where thoughts serenely sweet express
How pure, how dear their dwelling-place.

And on that cheek, and o'er that brow,
So soft, so calm, yet eloquent,
The smiles that win, the tints that glow,
But tell of days in goodness spent,
A mind at peace with all below,
A heart whose love is innocent!

Lord Byron

QUIET MOMENTS

EACH time I feel the sunlight's kiss,
I close my eyes and reminisce,
And I think of times of long ago,
And of the folks I used to know,
My school friends "Ginger", George and Jim,
The local baths where we would swim,
Summer camps beneath the stars,
Prized newts and sticklebacks in jars,
The smell of Mother's baking bread,
The cocoa when I went to bed,
Those castles out of sand we made,
The games of cricket that we played,
Punch and Judy, donkey rides,
The fairground helter skelter slides,
When I was young and in my prime,
And unaware of passing time.
But now I'm old with time to spare,
To sit in my reclining chair,
Where in a quiet moment's bliss,
I close my eyes and reminisce.

Brian H. Gent

SUNFLOWERS

AT my pollen-powdered table
I sit in idle admiration,
Becalmed in the balmy air,
Sunstruck by helianthus.

Fired by summer's blinding glare
they blaze, dazzle and hum,
this shock of sunflowers
with refulgent, apricot eyes.

Haloed in heat-haze they flare
and flashlight brazenly down
on the dust-glazed yard,
thresh the glitter of earthshine.

While pampered hens lazily pick
at the winking, white-hot grit,
or pluck at grass-fleams gleaned
from between sun-baked flags.

John Ellis

SEA WIND

THE plaintive voice of the sea wind sings
Of long ago forgotten things.
He whispers secrets, hopes and fears
And memories of far off years.

Then growing fresher, blowing strong,
He sweeps the clouds and waves along.
He whips the spray and scatters sand,
And tosses pebbles on the land.

In quiet mood he sings once more
Of ebbing tide and distant shore.
And in my mind I drift along,
I travel with the sea wind's song.

Iris Hesselden

A BIRTHDAY

MY heart is like a singing bird
Whose nest is in a water'd shoot;
My heart is like an apple-tree
Whose boughs are bent with thick-set fruit;
My heart is like a rainbow shell
That paddles in a halcyon sea;
My heart is gladder than all these,
Because my love is come to me.
Raise me a dais of silk and down;
Hang it with vair and purple dyes;
Carve it in doves and pomegranates,
And peacocks with a hundred eyes;
Work it in gold and silver grapes,
In leaves and silver fleur-de-lys;
Because the birthday of my life
Is come, my love is come to me.

Christina Georgina Rossetti

SCHIEHALLION

TONIGHT the moon rose in a blue sky.
It was almost eleven, June over,
The sun warm enough to walk in even then;
The river beyond the trees a slow, white slide,
Reflecting its whispered journey to the sea.

The moon rose over the hills, butter yellow,
Rippled upwards through sleeves of cloud.
I felt suddenly a yearning to be gone, to leave
The safe familiarity of the town's days.

And walk the mountain then, that night,
Walk the brittle whiteness of it, the sheer upwards edge
Into a clear sky, an open mouth of moonlight,
A peak lit crystal in the summer night –
Windless and magic.

Kenneth C. Steven

98

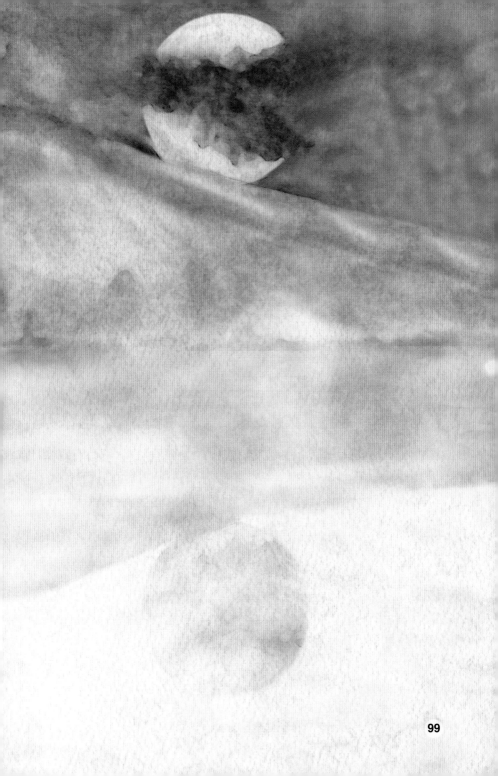

JUNE SHOWER

A LITTLE light rain
Fell,
Unblocked
The night-time air,
Released a cocktail mix
High
On honeysuckle,
Mock orange,
Rose.

A little light rain
Fell,
Gave way
To showers of scent,
Refunded in part
Summer's stipend,
This perfumed air,
Unbottled,
Free of price.

David Elder

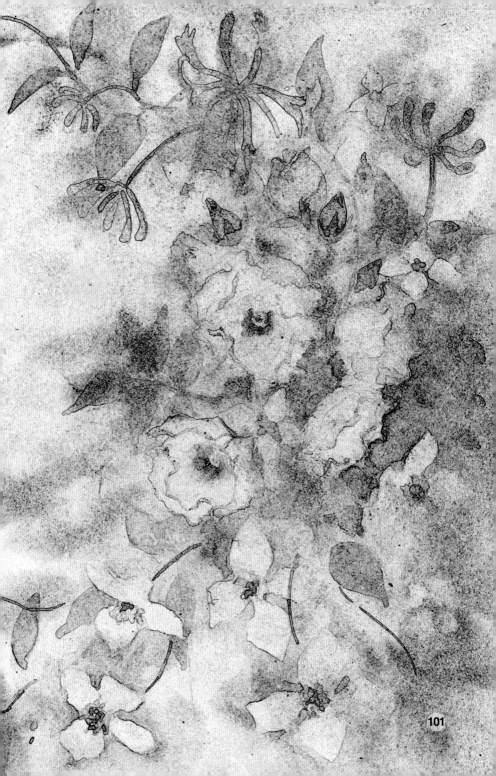

LARKSPUR SUMMER

IT was warm in the mornings of my
larkspur summer
I would jump the clump of scarlet peonies
And run down to the fruit trees to count the
apples
After the June drop, making sure of the crop
Before surveying my larkspur in their beds.
Their delicate shades delighted me,
I gently plucked the dead away, and cleaned
The cuckoo spit from the tendrils of their
greenery.
I cared for them, and shared them with my
mother.
On damp days they glowed against the
darkened fence
As I pulled weeds from their slender stems
And waited for the seed pods to ripen.
I thought I would have another larkspur
summer
By planting the seeds of the summer before.
But nothing stays the same; I was on the edge
of childhood,
On a path leading to adolescence,
Yet, in a corner of my mind
The innocence of that summer prevails.

Drina Brokenbrow

SUMMER SOLSTICE EVENING

ALONG a road scarce-travelled,
Stretching out to nothingness,
We strolled in the dimming light
Of the longest day.
Late, late at dusk
When, into the field edge,
The white wisp of a barn owl
Drifted silently,
Flapping a feathered fan
Soft as silk,
Yet carrying still
In its undercarriage
An airborne weapon
Concealed,
Waiting to surprise.

David Elder

A WEB OF DREAMS

I HEARD the strumming of the wild woodpecker
As I stood beside the flowing stream,
The gentle lap of water,
The faint whistling of tiny birds
And the pheasant's call
All seemed to weave a web of dreams
About my soul
Till I no longer trod the tired earth
But seemed transported to a place
Where spring's sweet birth
Had wakened songs of joy —
And I stood transfixed,
Happy as a freckled boy
About his play.
A blackbird sang
Above the fields and
I went on my way
Rejoicing.

Jenny Whybrow

BUTTERCUPS

THE spun gold of childhood
 Gathered into a posy of reminiscence.
Bright treasury of recollection
Blowing among forgotten footpaths,
Where half-remembered faces
Smile and beckon from distant meadows
Gleaming with petal-light.
Dark leaves to lay restraint
Upon the vivid coinage of yellow blooms.
Tacky gold-dust of pollen
Clinging to sills and fingertips
With the persistence of morning light
Across a landscape
Still wrapped in yesterday's shadows.

Joan Howes

GLASGOW KINDLING 1951

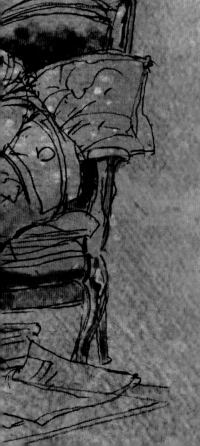

IN quilted nests, on Gran's leatherette chair,
We watch the ritual lighting of the fire;
The cold ash raked and rusted bars crushed clean,
Best cinders put aside to use again.
Her work-smooth fingers, knuckled large with age,
Make folds and twists of last week's news,
Neat braids called paper sticks.
My sister's hair she wove this way, and that,
In deft plaits of muted love.

The taper sets a hesitating flame
She blows with gentle breath to bring to life,
First curling brown, then guttering yellow light;
The walls draw back and shadows edge away;
She turns her head, the north-blue eyes meets ours
And smile with rare uncensored pleasure.

Mike Cobban

TWO HILLS ABOVE THE HASTE

TO have trekked above Craigmead
in a summer evening of skylarks
when they rocket out of the tussocks
tuning their notes as they climb

To have made for a sun soon to drop
on the shoulder of West Lomond
as the land to your left falls away
to a glistering Forth below

To have stood knee deep in bracken
in the shade of Falkland Hill,
panning around a breathless plain
from Freuchie to Auchtermuchty,
tracing the shores and shipping lanes
from Bass Rock to Burntisland

From a high spot look over the rooftops,
there's an invite warmly extended
by two sisters, unchanging and sovereign,
and the humbler slopes beneath

Map it well now for more than one pathway
leads into the Lomond adventure.
step out with an eager tread then go
with grace in the bosom of Fife.

Ian Nimmo White

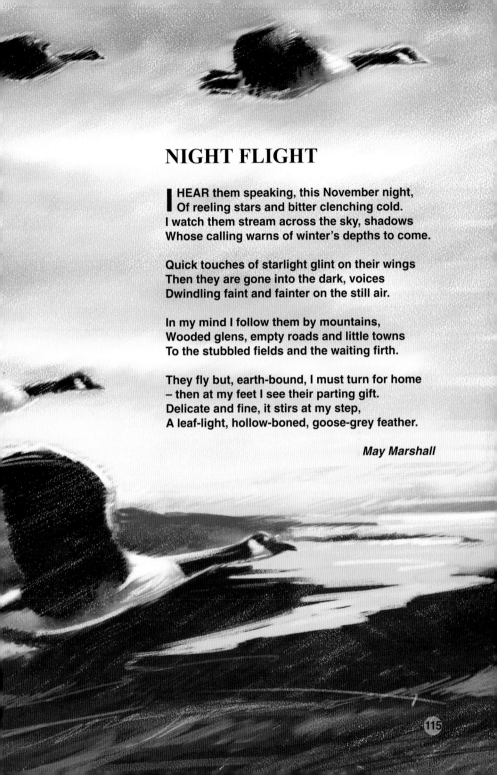

NIGHT FLIGHT

I HEAR them speaking, this November night,
Of reeling stars and bitter clenching cold.
I watch them stream across the sky, shadows
Whose calling warns of winter's depths to come.

Quick touches of starlight glint on their wings
Then they are gone into the dark, voices
Dwindling faint and fainter on the still air.

In my mind I follow them by mountains,
Wooded glens, empty roads and little towns
To the stubbled fields and the waiting firth.

They fly but, earth-bound, I must turn for home
– then at my feet I see their parting gift.
Delicate and fine, it stirs at my step,
A leaf-light, hollow-boned, goose-grey feather.

May Marshall

WINTERSONG

WIND from the Nor'nor'west
  Curdles the sea tonight,
Yellow foam rolls up the shingled shore
From breakers crested tight
And curled like wayward locks of hair
On an ancient pate turned white.

Wind from the Nor'nor'west
Carries the winter in,
Chasing the last migrating bird,
Rattling hail on tin
Roofs, slates and window panes;
Shivering those within.

Wind from the Nor'nor'west,
Pulling at hearth and fire,
Whispering threats beneath the door,
Sagging the telephone wire,
Driving sheep behind the wall,
Whirling the cock on the byre.

Wind from the Nor'nor'west
Harries the year away,
Flattens brown reeds and the last long grass.
Nothing remains to say
The land will ever see Spring again,
The sky so hung with grey.

Iain Dubh

BACK GARDENS (CRAIL)

AMONG a crush of bikes and creels,
Onions hang from blackened sheds,
Poles mark out trim drying greens.

From orange or green lines of rope,
Sheets droop like wintered sails,
Prayer flags of pink and lemon.

Pigeons coo in dark lofts,
A sleepy cat half eyes a thrush
Tap, tap tapping a hard shell.

Barrows stand marooned by steaming
Middens, cabbages crinkle their purple
Leaves against the frosted soil.

Ice settles on an enamelled pail,
As blue tits hammer a coconut bell
And foghorns boom far out to sea.

Ruth Walker

119

DEER

THEY are there in the darkness,
In the warm night and the warm shadows;
Such big softness you must hold your breath
To know they're there. In lamplight they loom large,
The budded tips of their antlers jagging the air,
Eyes lemoned in the light.

Yet break a branch
And they've leapt away,
Vanished as soft as thistledown,
Gone into the umber night as one,
The fields left eerie and empty behind them
As a gourd of moon spills from the opened dark.

Kenneth C. Steven

120

EVENING REFLECTIONS

AS darkness steals across the sky
And evening fades to night
Across the lake the moonbeams make
A path of silvery light.
The water with its lapping sound
Which beats against the shale
Mirrors in its rippled face
The moonlight soft and pale.

The reeds and rushes on the banks
Are bathed in eerie glow
Listening to the voices of
The tides which ebb and flow.
The wind is sighing in the trees
As branches bend and sway
And on the birches' satin gowns
The shadows interplay.

And in the distance from the hills
Night creatures call and cry
Their echoes caught up in the breeze
As it goes trembling by.
And all around there is a sense
Of calm tranquillity
As nature seems to hold the night
In peaceful harmony.

Kathleen Gillum

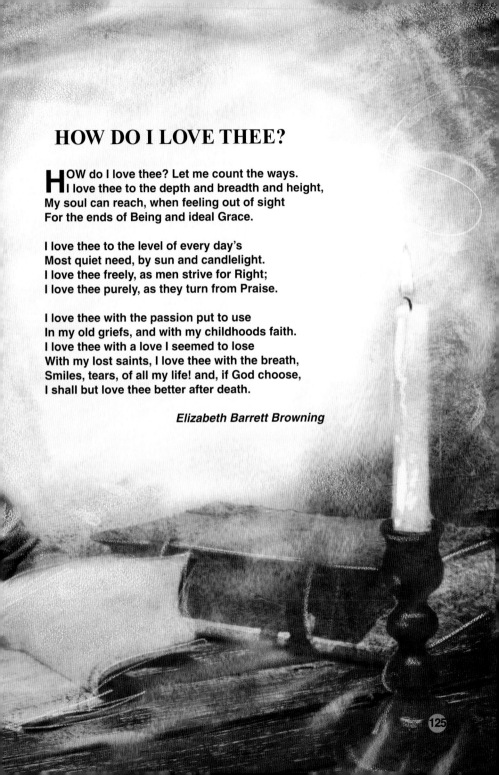

HOW DO I LOVE THEE?

HOW do I love thee? Let me count the ways.
I love thee to the depth and breadth and height,
My soul can reach, when feeling out of sight
For the ends of Being and ideal Grace.

I love thee to the level of every day's
Most quiet need, by sun and candlelight.
I love thee freely, as men strive for Right;
I love thee purely, as they turn from Praise.

I love thee with the passion put to use
In my old griefs, and with my childhoods faith.
I love thee with a love I seemed to lose
With my lost saints, I love thee with the breath,
Smiles, tears, of all my life! and, if God choose,
I shall but love thee better after death.

Elizabeth Barrett Browning

LISTENING

DEEP down in sea pools
Restless rhythms ripple out
From ancient mystery ways,
Set by sea, sun and moon
Known to fish and birds,
By herds and hunters traced
Between ice ebb and ice flow,
That from farthest star flow
Require our constant listening.

Paul Turner

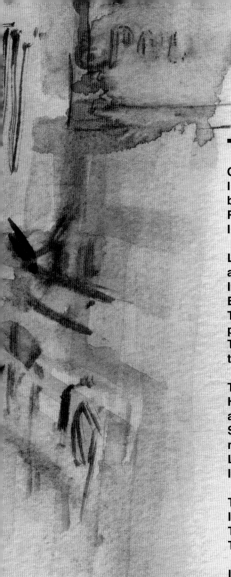

SHOES

THE shoemaker stitched and sewed
In the dark scent of his own world.
Once a year
I went in there, to the black adverts for
boots and polish
Rusty over the walls of his shop.
I blinked

Like something that had tumbled down
a hole
Into the hearth of the earth.
Even the air was tanned,
The chestnut of shoes burnished and
perfect from hands
That had poured in the pure oils of
their love,

Their labour.
He wiped those huge hands on his
apron,
Stood as I smoothed my feet into the
mended shoes,
Looking, his eyes life a calf's, brown
In an air that was brown, a brown cave.

The scent of leather hung in the air
In my shoes that were as good as new
That fitted my feet like hooves –
They shone so I saw my own smile.

I went out into the blue breeze of the
springtime
Watching my step, all the way home.
Still,
School scuffed them and skinned
them,
Reduced them at last to a shadow of
all they had been.

Kenneth C. Steven

129

THE OCEAN ABOVE

MAYBE when the day's seawork
And the day's skywork are done,
After finely frayed moorit cloudstrands
Have tassel-teased waves with rain,
Smudging the last strokes of gold
Fading down from crimson and rose,
Somewhere beyond the grey line
Where my eye says there are islands,
The ocean above and the one below
Finally embrace to reflect and to play
The game that will shape another day.

Paul Turner

ANOTHER AUTUMN

PURPLE lips,
a tang that lingers,
juice on my sweater,
thorns in my fingers.

Homemade pie
and a giggling wine,
field mice and thrushes
and autumn sunshine.

Scarlet scratches
in a golden haze.
Yes, I remember
those blackberry days.

Gerald Hampshire

MEMORIES...

WITHIN this shell;
A churning wave,
A seagull's call,
A happy child.

Within this shell;
The salt-tang breeze,
The sandy bay,
The rising cliffs.

Within this shell –
My souvenirs ...

Elizabeth Gozney

STARLINGS

EACH evening, they arrive
To serrate the sky-line
Then tear off to town
In a wheeling, diving, soaring
Stretch of starlings.
On buses and trains
Commuters cannot see
chiaroscuro made by birds
Above the Clyde:
Dark, liquid cloud transposed with light
As starlings settle for the night
To stack a steeple
Or bulge a bridge.

John McInnes

THE LINE TO WICK AND THURSO

NORTH of Inverness the land changes –
Turns wildcat, heather root and hill,
Miles of everywhere, rivers blethering from glens,
Empty ruins staring from hills like ghosts.
Stags battle away from the train,
Vanish into thin mist.

This land that belonged to the pearlfisher
The crofter, the laird, the poacher –
Who does it belong to now?
Who can own ruggedness
Or an eagle curling the sky?

Kenneth C. Steven

139

A MARATHON ASCENT

IN quest of the summit,
Walkers marvel as strings of mist
Unravel over a maze of contours,
Snagging in dark horns or oak and beech.

Ancient Gods live here, or heroes.
Their knuckles crack in the clack
Of stones grey as their swords
Sent hurtling by boot-shod feet;
Bracken togas their mud-dark flesh
Or shields it with the softness of moss;
Their battle roar blisters bark with lichen.

A mountainous Narcissus,
Ben Vane admires its reflection
Of russet, gold and green, slashed with waterfalls,
Holding its breath to prevent unseemly ripples;
Boulders break Loch Lubnaig, a memorial cairn,
While Echo's tears drip from birch and alder.

Rowena M. Love

ON CREAG NA COIREACH

WHILE out walking the upper slopes
We came across a hare,
Stone-still its silhouette
Half-sunken in heather,
Trying hard to forget primal fear.

Its ears like eyes
Had mapped our coming,
And now its racing heart
Willed the wind
To whisk us far from here.

A game of Statues
Or was it Risk?
But then exploding into life
It fled to play
A different game…

A game of Hide and Seek.

David Elder

THE BRIGHT MOMENT

ALL day the rain out of the west,
The telegraph wires looping through the mist,
Lambs lying wet in the edges of ditches,
Shivering, their mothers beside them like old stone.

We walked into the wind,
Fought our way to the loch
That fluttered and flamed, gusted greys and blacks –
And there on the water, together, two swans
Rising at our coming, flagging the wind,
Held together by the wind, those big buffetings –
Head and neck, head and neck, coupled
In the grey rambling of the sky.

And in that moment
I thought that nothing we had done or ever did
Could compare with this, this mastery of the sky, this storm dance –
And all I wanted always was to watch them.

Kenneth Steven

146

A NEW DAY

So here hath been dawning
Another blue day;
Think, wilt thou let it
Slip useless away?

Out of Eternity
This new day is born;
Into Eternity
At night will return.

Behold it aforetime
No eye ever did;
So soon it forever
From all eyes is hid.

Here hath been dawning
Another blue day;
Think, wilt thou let it
Slip useless away?

Thomas Carlyle

LOOKING SHARP

WINTER'S first barbaric breath
Resounds on the flintrock path
That climbs to the lap of Falkland Hill

Where the last few switching swallows
Are making manoeuvres so fast
Their colours can't be seen.

An ember of red, what's left
Of the setting sun, is pouched
By a cloud on the Western Hill,

And with a Caribbean speed
Dusk embraces. Birdsong too
Will fade when the spooks move in.

Ian Nimmo White

THE WIND THAT SHAKES THE BARLEY

THERE'S music in my heart all day,
I hear it late and early,
It comes from fields are far away,
The wind that shakes the barley.

Above the uplands drenched with dew
The sky hangs soft and pearly,
An emerald world is listening to
The wind that shakes the barley.

Above the bluest mountain crest
The lark is singing rarely,
It rocks the singer into rest,
The wind that shakes the barley.

Oh, still through summers and through springs
It calls me late and early.
Come home, come home, come home, it sings,
The wind that shakes the barley.

Katharine Tynan

FLOW COUNTRY

WE pass the last garden
A deserted swing and sodden washing
The flagstone dyke marking the boundary
Between smoothed-out fields
And tightly-woven heather
Then a high deer fence etched black against the twilight
And row on row of fir trees on the march.

Late October and the rowans wait
Leafless already
By a ruined croft.

I wish I could reach out
And touch the stillness
And take the curving road
That leads towards the turreted hunting lodge
Lying shuttered under a silver of moon.

And as we shudder to a halt at a request stop
A silvered owl takes flight
Across the wilderness.

Liz Carew

153

TWELVE O'CLOCK

SIX boots tramp like hooves at the back door,
Come in to the room's warm glare, the ready table.

Pieces of broken talk, a folded newspaper, scraped chairs;
Grave a scattering of words, a murmur of amens.

Then spilt potatoes, soft and flowery, for bits of butter,
And poured glasses full of sudden sunlight,

As light slides out from late September cloud,
Glinting the knives, rosing the turned faces –

No sound except the somewhere song of a tap's drip
And down the hall a radio left talking to itself.

Kenneth C. Steven

SEPTEMBER

WHEN summertime is weary
And evening comes too soon,
Then August will limp away,
Beneath the waxen moon.
And September will enter,
Just like a regal queen,
To drift across the shoreline,
Where many crowds have been.
She passes by the flowers
That have been summer's crown,
And sees their fragile petals,
Slowly meander down.
Her laughter gently breezes
Across the fields of green
Where once the fruits of summer,
In their splendour were seen.
And just before she settles,
She seems to pause awhile
To watch August sadly turn
And give a farewell smile.
Then she rests upon the earth,
Her fragrances will stay
Until October enters,
But that's another day.

Mo Crawshaw

AUBADE

EARLIEST sun has kissed
The cliff-top, breaking through
Lingering scarfs of mist
Re-opening the view.
Sea still as rippled glass,
Quietness so profound,
Tide pausing as I pass.
Never the slightest sound
As night rolls back – remark
How islands gleam anew.
A solitary lark
Sings out, breaking through
Last silence of the dark.
Is this not holy ground?

Iain Dubh

THE LOVELY

ON a night so clear the darkness rang with stars
that shone and shivered as they sang
of tumbling down to decorate the trees,
I saw their brilliant faces watching me.
Their lovely shapes were sewn across the sky,
some pinned along the fraying edge, some high,
and when the wind reached up to snatch their gilt
it seemed I heard their silvery laughter lilt.
Alone among the thoughts of heaven bared,
of which no graceful wonder had been spared,
I waited until dawn arose; I stayed
until the last bright spangle fell away.

Rachel Wallace-Oberle

THE LAST END

THE scents of night perfume the air,
The shadows longer grow.
The rink is hushed, the match depends
Upon the final throw.

It's played! A word of praise for him
Who made the vital shot
A social glass, then home we go,
All rivalries forgot.

I don't care very much if I
Don't reach life's richest goals
If fame and fortune meant that I'd
Forfeit my game of bowls.

D. Hope

SO SWEET LOVE SEEMED

So sweet love seemed that April morn,
When first we kissed beside the thorn,
So strangely sweet, it was not strange
We thought that love could never change.

But I can tell – let truth be told –
That love will change in growing old;
Though day by day is naught to see,
So delicate his motions be.

And in the end 'twill come to pass
Quite to forget what once he was,
Nor even in fancy to recall
The pleasure that was all in all.

His little spring, that sweet we found,
So deep in summer floods is drowned,
I wonder bathed in joy complete,
How love so young could be so sweet.

Robert Bridges

MIST-COVERED MOUNTAIN

ON this day when good views are forecast
A thick mist hung heavily over Lochnagar.
We set out to find the path,
A dotted line that wriggled our intent
Across contours and symbols of scree;
But by Meikle Pap the corrie wall
Still remained just a myth,
A half-imagined edge;
Whilst at the top of The Ladder
A bouldered blockade buried our gaze.

Reaching the summit tor the day darkened more
And it was only along the Glas Allt, descending,
That white-spumed waterfalls sparkled some light.
Zig-zagging down to the loch's shoreline
We returned to the Spittal of Glenmuick,
Where, glancing skyward once more,
We saw the summit — clear and fine,
Mist-free and bathed
In the evening light
Of heavenly blue.

David Elder

THE BIRNAM OAK

WE thread our way along the river
Towards Dunkeld.
Around us mountains with jagged edges
Are shutting out the light.
Bushes jostle.
Roots trip us up.
Rich black mud sucks at our shoes.
Dusk is falling until
Time rewinds and we are in a sunlit meadow.
Here stands the Birnam Oak
A wide-girthed trunk and burnished canopy
Outlined against a milky sky
And aisles of rosebay willowherb.

A notice proclaims the oak's great age
Its noble fight against the ranks of conifers
Marching down sleep slopes towards the Tay
That Shakespeare may have visited the area
With a troop of English players.
I wonder.

Seek answers from the oak's pitted, peeling bark
From its ancient limbs propped up by crutches
From its whispering leaves
Know I will have to go back
To the text.

Liz Carew

ON THE EDGE

STANDING to attention
Shoulder to shoulder,
Black against white,
White against black

The b & w guillemots
Of the Bass Rock
Claim more than
Squatting rights

Practising some banter,
Walking the auk talk,
Feeding and preening,
Or cleaning out

Their two-by-twos
On the ledge just living
For the moment
On the edge.

David Elder

EMBERS OF THE DAY

THE burning cinder of the sun
Descends with rosy glow
Upon the red horizon's rim
Suspended deep and low.
A giant orb of crimson fire
Like some eternal eye,
Casts out its rays of radiant flame
Across the evening sky.
And as the sun sinks in the west
And disappears from sight,
The dying embers of the day
Merge softly with the night.

Kathleen Gillum

The Artists Are:-

James Dewar
Front cover, Visit Woodland, Aquainted With Autumn,
Seasonal Wisdom, Birch In Winter, Winter!, February Thoughts,
Portrait Of Spring, Lupin, Willow Cottage, Sunset Over The Sea,
The Garden, The May Path, Night Flight, Deer,
How Do I Love Thee?, Flow Country, End Papers.

David Matysiak
Secrets Of The Night, Special Love, The Good Morning,
Benison, Sea Wind, A Birthday, Larkspur Summer,
Summer Solstice Evening, A Web Of Dreams,
Glasgow Kindling, Inside Cover (fireplace).

Mandy Murray
Gold, Clocks Away, Winter Limes, Yippee!, Ice Breakers,
Quiet Moments, Listening, Ocean Above, Memories, Starlings,
Twelve O'Clock, September, The Lovely.

Amanda Dixon
Love Is..., Encounter, The Elfin Fair, Winter Sprite,
Spring Garland, Hills Above, Evening Reflection, New Day,
Looking Sharp, The Wind That Shakes The Barley,
On The Edge, Embers Of The Day.

Helen Welsh
September Song, The Stream, Hebridean Reflection,
Dry Dock, This Day, The Frogs' Return, Sparkle, A Field In Fife,
Faery Land, Seal At Kintyre, A Red, Red Rose,
Buttercup Bower, She Walks In Beauty, Sunflowers,
Schiehallion, June Shower, Buttercups, Back Gardens Crail,
Another Autumn, On Creag Na Coireach, Bright Moment,
Aubade, Mist Covered Mountain, Birnam Oak.

Kirk Houston
The Last End, So Sweet Love Seemed.

Inglis Thorburn
Photo Of A Dear Friend.

Norma Maclean
The Salmon's Return, Winter Song, Shoes,
The Line To Wick And Thurso, Marathon Ascent.